A TOAST IN THE HOUSE OF FRIENDS

A Toast in the House of Friends

POEMS

Akilah Oliver

COFFEE HOUSE PRESS

Minneapolis, Minnesota :: 2009

COFFEE HOUSE PRESS books are available to the trade through our primary distributor, Consortium Book Sales & Distribution, www.cbsd.com or (800) 283-3572. For personal orders, catalogs, or other information, write to: info@coffeehousepress.org.

Coffee House Press is a nonprofit literary publishing house. Support from private foundations, corporate giving programs, government programs, and generous individuals helps make the publication of our books possible. We gratefully acknowledge their support in detail in the back of this book.

To you and our many readers around the world, we send our thanks
for your continuing support.

LIBRARY OF CONGRESS CIP INFORMATION

Oliver, Akilah.
A toast in the house of friends : poems / by Akilah Oliver.
p. cm.
ISBN 978-1-56689-222-3 (alk. paper)
I. Title.
PS3565.L4575T63 2008
811'.54—DC22
2008012531

PRINTED IN THE U.S.A.

ACKNOWLEDGMENTS

Some of these poems were published in: *Not for Mothers Only: Contemporary Poems on Child-Getting and Child-Rearing, Bombay Gin, The Recluse, Encyclopedia, Chain, nocturnes, Blood & Tears: Poems for Matthew Shepard, The Poetry Project Newsletter,* and *EOAGH.*

"An Arriving Guard of Angels, Thusly Coming to Greet" appeared as a limited edition chapbook. Warm thanks to Farfalla Press, Anne Waldman, Tyler Burba, Steven Taylor, Latasha N. Nevada Diggs, Todd Burba, and the many writers and musicians who collaborated on the evolution and presentation of this work.

Gratitude to the LINKS Community Network friends who fought the good fight to raise awareness of the need for humane, universal health care: Karen Zorn, Ellen Maslow, Marda Kirn, Josh Hershman, Christopher Lites, Nick Houy, and the many others who volunteered and contributed.

& on behalf of Oluchi McDonald, I'd like to thank his friends for their love. & to the ASSHOLES, may you continue to paint in one form or another.

For my son Oluchi, brother Marc, my mother,
and the dear loved ones who held the space of this house.

Contents

In Aporia

"I realized everything I was doing must have been Death. It was Christmas or Labor Day—a holiday—and every time you turned on the radio they said something like 'four million' or 'going to die.'"
—ANDY WARHOL

I'm trying on egos, [a justification for the planet's continuance]. Oh hello transgressor, you've come to collect utilitarian debts, humbling narrative space. Give me a condition and wheatgrass,

I his body is disintegrating, I his body is ossification. Death my habit radius, yeah yeah.
I his body can't refuse this summons. I can't get out
this fucking room. Tell me something different about torture
dear Trickster.

Tell me about the lightness *my mother told me to pick the one i love the best*
how it signals everything I ever wish to believe true just holy on my ship.
I jump all over this house. this is it [what i thought is thought only,
nothing more deceptive than]:
I his body keeps thinking someone will come along, touch me.
As like human. Or lima bean.

I'm cradling you to my breast, you are looking out. A little wooden lion you & Peter carve on Bluff Street is quieting across your cheekbone. Not at all like the kind of terror found in sleep, on trembling grounds.

It is yesterday now. I have not had a chance to dance in this century.
Tonight I shall kill someone,
a condition to remember Sunday mornings.

To think of lives as repetitions [rather than singular serial incarnations].
To understand your death is as exacerbating as trying to figure out why
as schoolchildren in mid-nineteen-sixties Southern California we
performed reflexive motions:
cutting out lace snowflakes, reading Dick and Jane search for their
missing mittens,
imagining snow.

And this too, fiction. The book I would want to right.
The restored fallen, heroic.

Did you expect a different grace from the world? Or upon exit?

I'm working on "tough." They think I am already. All ready.

Who is the dead person? Is "I'm sorry" real to a dead person?
Browning grass. My hands on this table. A contentious century.
A place to pay rent. Redemptive moments.

Am I now the dead person?
Dead person, dead person, will you partake in my persimmon feast?

The body inside the body astounds, confesses sins of the funhouse.

I too have admired the people of this planet.
Their frilly, ordered intellects.
The use they've made of cardamom,
radiation as well. How they've pasteurized milk, loaned surnames to stars,
captured tribes, diseases, streets, and ideas too.

the standstill world

time, my favorite escapee, tricks, appears as
narrator, then a broken brake coil, then
fifty, now know it's sixty-five, now it's seventy
children burned, top floor nursery, the Kumbakonam temple town,
southern India region, where is today, back in a parking lot,
would you buy, a brown messiah, reproduced on a white hoodie,
oh my, her grandson shies in her fervor, it is cute, black market
deals produced as scripts, between lights the
folly mistress, she thinks of some card games,
we might want to play to rope in clients, i think i
am admired, but the runners are stopping their
steroids & quitting, the Sudanese government is complicit,
the refugees are in Chad now, or Jordan wants one hundred fifty
thousand for one year's stay, a way to measure the life
span of rubble, once the family home, i have an
empty book bag for you to put these tales in,
see i am a griot collector now, i tell you these things are happening,
the complicity, the rubble, the scripts, the money,
the burns, the runners, the lights, the deals,
all circular errors, each so fixed, real, & also traces,
blushing moments

laughter from the altar

we were all familiars in the obscenity of cities,

and to be gentle here, perhaps not so obscure

and to labor in a snail state, a minstrelsy disco

and to seek refuge, a spinning wheel at the fair

and to dive into the otherwise, breaking the fast

and to derogate the holy sentence, tongues spied

and to give thanks, my cousins bear me no ill will

and to define nothing, myself a willing accomplice

and to tender down the wayward slope, a loved boy

and to have leverage, like on occasion we did before

and to silence come early, this dawn abundant in blue

and to perform the ragged hip dance, i name you again

and to purvey the scene, a hawker of rhinestone trinkets

and to slip unnoticed, in clean swipes of brazen undercut

and to carouse with strangers, a feast of trains embarking

and to honor thy mother and father, this faded polaroid test and to lazy the afternoon, the thunderous applauding infants

and to linger by the turnstile at noon, an unattended landscape

and to shadow my flight across the threshold, an exiled goddess

and to ply my trade without complaint, a wispy gone benediction

and to not judge me, when i take my counsel from singeing addicts

and to bury a placenta in an ashen grove, a bold rapping of knuckles

and to know officious failings place holds, as some kind of looseness

and to wile unscathed under a dunce's cap, each oared in her own birth

and to chute from the heavenly morgue, an inconstant arrival of dimples

and to white out within the imperial gaze, a colonnade of violets sentient

and to chase traces across borrowed pastures, a movie reel viewed asleep

and to homage the young men, stepping purposely in Johnny Hartman voice

and to disquiet the armies of disused spears, a brokerage in the damp shade

and to privilege the body as supplicant unescorted, everywhere a flailing limb

and to speak easy in voices delivered from postcards, no one amongst us pure

and to ride the two-wheeler to crisscross the storm, a titled vandal in long pants

and to be born with a full suit of aces, these things i remember in the gilded hour

and to show not fear when faced with thine enemies, a toast in the house of friends

go

often now when i imagine life i think of what should
be finite, the guise of limitability, the desire for stop

are there greeters there [are you one] when we former ghosts arrive

is this sea deceptive, as if alive or an   actor, the world masked

in my own way there was a time when i stumbled over a tense: says/said
now, bereft, in anticipation of how night collapses
into its own effluence i conjugate occasions, ask just for time, just a little time,
to get love right

disguise

mimetic mouth full of cotton,
wandering through Sheol,
do you come offering sword and peppermint tea,
do i receive you as nemesis, as concession,
as goat.

is there soup in this sugar house, a hearth
to set a fire, a single bare bulb for comfort,
the lord of parachutes.

Chinook winds are outside blowing, lying.
i allow this jungle.

under that tree, where the cat has tagged the bark,
that's where i hunt

grace

"They shall
utah ocher
speak of the glory
a stellar sight for any
initiated or not
i heard
that there
a lady
did speak
of finer
things to come
she offered
you accepted
a pear,
     though it was not
yet ripe
     for the ride over
of Your kingdom,
is it like a big thing, this glory
is it like a simple lightsome or period or minus sign
and talk of your power"
         it is marketable, yes, i believe it has been marketed,
      sold on a common block, ice cubes, and crumbled dynasties as legacy,
        is it small and black, this power
"He counts the number of the stars;
     by vocation i shall call my brother
parachutist,

     by desire i shall call my mother
minor god,
     by birthright i shall call my father
salesman,
He calls them all by name."
  by luck i shall call myself
poet,
   by design i shall call my son
painter,
     by wish i shall call that bright spot there,   lingering past the din,
twin
"Men ate angels' food;
& it is
bittersweet
& this cup
is full &
marked
He sent them food to the full."
by tender
prints
i would
not offer
it away

                                  Have you
                   travailed far?

                   Have you been to Bashan?
"But it was you, a man my equal, my companion and my acquaintance
lost, i lost you on the way to deliverance or
i bowed out,
 my lover, my betrayer, my staff,

my neither, my holder of chokes

                ————it is only faintly some mornings, i remember the
fold of your body————
We took sweet counsel together, and walked to the house of God in the throng."
how silly
it all
seems now
but when
i thought
of it then
we were both
so immediate

Italicized lines are from Psalms 145:11, Psalms 147:4, Psalms 78:25,
Psalms 55:13, Psalms 55:14.

wishes

i do want to be soft,
hold a given name as if it were lover,
cultivate horehound to feed neuroses in troubled times,
allow some hoopla in these rooms.

i could couldn't i

temper heresy with a friend of mine,
be measured & fortified,
laugh at nothing discernible,
myself be prescient dreamer busy with wines,
a wearer of henna ankhs,
an old soul & sometimes the innocent fool,
irrationally content alongside the girning rain.

dissolving frames

in renewal   of pledge

we   are finding our way

his one perfect body   radiating a whiskey night

the why of things that go   the angry dispossessed queen prepares   often found

receding   launches all the resources of her shabby empire

          the seriously coy

make an escape today   gatekeepers asleep on duty

we lose another chance   as valuable

walking along smith street   consciously looking down to register

territories   narrow, which is like the foyer

                    fleetingly i thought i had hurt him

going along with the play   i remember every morality tale

          see you in various incinerated days   what is it like

when your virginal witness   begins to drift away

the dollar store on jefferson & western avenue   we ride past on great elephants,

unlike any other beasts   fully engaged in this

false translation   at daybreak the voucher is lost   this is nothing is

          grand central market has fish on sale

pop&mockery

if in fact: this much sorrow is too much sadness

]sadness: then+
who might be@com taking me for a ride—

i bet there are forests out there
and an imagination lies dormant so the equation is un/decipherable
or there
is not an expected outcome to the =
everywhere the signs should have been apparent
was i not chosen & mystics so overrated
i hate the world

i am so intrinsically of the wor/ld
do you call that deceiver *god* except after "c"

why was shirley temple's added surname "black" how did this mockery
and marriage legitimize all the post/possibility (ambassador to ghana—
where art thou nkrumah) of deliverance / this is not the word i mean to
use to disclaim / language is leaving me: ahhhhh—this victimization shit
is not stable and the victors:
when are we going to safari
we: [astounded exclamation]
nancy reagan out of my head

if you were here we would have spaghetti dinner the sun would set pretty
because i would make it
safe ha ha

in temples

to sit, to sit with it   Here, to swallow this morning's sweet dull deliverance, I cast
the mother back into more primitive light. I offer mortal lullaby to you good
Lord of Miniature Bruises. What did you teach on grace, speech-making, pythons,
eros, while I was out counting skulls?

    How human fragility

    How war liturgies

    How to be a rock star among Republicans

the trace of what cremated godhead is this moving through Me, strewn & plundered,
there's more dead than I can count already, these formidable no bodies. Is there a name
for all this noise.

milady

what would I ask
of lover?
to come to here
whispering with ghosts?
to sit enthralled in
vanishings?
to detonate & plummet
in apparent form?
to come to
foreign brouhaha?
to witness this
breaking?

yes, milady, to be my observer,
in this, my fait accompli

ache

at my purest once,
in response to *what do you want*
i said,
i said i just want to know god

second sight

and this is the way I thought it would be:

                                     each trance leading to another not unlike

serial escalators,

     the miracle a suspended verdict

untested.   a biographical option

to wake in dark rooms, a slight chill ruminates.

the last ghost dies off before coffee

a kidnapped zapatista smokes american cigarettes behind the shower curtain,

two or three or thirteen

the inconsistency of numbers win the election

hyena (an absolution chant for the beloved community)

ashe ashe ashe ashe
how you say
ashe ashe ashe ashe
why you say
ashe ashe ashe ashe
which you say
ashe ashe ashe ashe
what you say
who you say

ohkay ohkay ohkay ohkay
how you do
ohkay ohkay ohkay ohkay
why you do
ohkay ohkay ohkay ohkay
which you do
ohkay ohkay ohkay ohkay
what you do
who you do

ayo ayo ayo ayo
why you want
ayo ayo ayo ayo
how you want
ayo ayo ayo ayo
which you want
ayo ayo ayo ayo

what you want
who you want

kikikiki kikikiki kikikiki
how you lie
kikikiki kikikiki kikikiki
which you lie
kikikiki kikikiki kikikiki
what you lie
kikikiki kikikiki kikikiki
why you lie
who you lie

olu olu olu olu
what you kill
olu olu olu olu
why you kill
olu olu olu olu
which you kill
olu olu olu olu
how you kill
who you kill

shalom shalom shalom shalom
why you hide
shalom shalom shalom shalom
how you hide
shalom shalom shalom shalom
which you hide
shalom shalom shalom shalom
what you hide
who you hide

selah selah selah selah
what you let down
selah selah selah selah
which you let down
selah selah selah selah
why you let down
selah selah selah selah
how you let down
who you let down

ye ye ye yemanya
why you trouble
ye ye ye yemanya
how you trouble
ye ye ye yemanya
what you trouble
ye ye ye yemanya
which you trouble
who you trouble

wadi wadi wadi wadi
which you love
wadi wadi wadi wadi
how you love
wadi wadi wadi wadi
why you love
wadi wadi wadi wadi
what you love
who you love

murdering

plot where he might lay his ambush down, christmas late past year,
fever clouds his visage, i to lace his frayed gluteus when chosen,
no hermetic task nice, granny's got a vintage shotgun attentive in closet.
i call for a sensorium before the last orders go out,
in accordance with his crazy lineage i can hear them pointing.

if i am to engage antiviolence work then by necessity i enter into contract
with violence,
no shy slipperies here.
it's just that, there is a turtle carrying its house on its back, the metaphor was put like
that once in little body time, and someone trying to knock it off,
the house that is, or the turtle, or the promises the house stands for,
this, what was ours invaded, defiled.

i to cord his frayed intestines when chosen.

yellow shirt

not mine
these legions of tees
not yours any longer
these vessel draperies
i keep

hauntings

some days appear as faces   the kind hiding its kin in furs,
myth faces,   faces miserly with kindness,
the types one might dream of murdering
in these mist days
when an act substitutes for an essence, nothing complete

hatchet

i work on stop if i am not, if you're not the yearning, glimpses of you,
my life, the things that are in it, the things that are not, but not the faces imprinted
everywhere, i'm dying with you
in our work, in your wanderings, in your
squabbles, our
dreams, your loving

settled

over with
being ashamed for
my life

in gray white waters

the stream, this dance with ghosts

                                        nothing done, defined, completed

perhaps no one
escapes this latched binary
except the unattached,
the dubious lucky

traveling

9/12/03
to mark transitions as balloons excavated.
move now.
what are twelves? what are nines? what are groups of subtraction?
johnny cash died today. your launch day.

9/13/03
today if we was talking, we would speak of Causality

9/15/03
as a spinster with nothing better to do, the window a pane of subtraction
adheres to this glancing late day trot, a record of waiting.
here in the forlorn majesty,
wizard should be capitalized, i wish there were a better castle,
uppercase flag.
today i fell on the way catching a bus. not really today.
but today i on the way i fail i
catching a bus. it is true in oakland once.

9/16/03
happy birthday.
and now, well now this action is prayer.
oh false clown face, oh how to reconcile the hours.
do you remember inside my body, how the quality of that day was so fretful,
empathetic too.

Crossover

(keep going)

when you left,
i mean when you had to go,
 —i intend an old saying,
when He called you home
(literally, as if jesus beckoned or something)
i was so unprepared for the earth's
grace as it disintegrated beneath me

: what is being found—
days = artificial temporal demarcations
sometimes moon
sky
your shape ephemeral & shy

a love language, that is:
a language gasping for consonants
shape the unspoken
as in: you are my first love, as in:
seeing eyes,
as in: you witnessed me
i wept you
or
when will i see you again—see,
like that,
a love language
      i
       you
       it is as hard as it seems
       i know you'd been crying

an arriving guard of angels, thusly coming
to greet

i am gasping at hosts

dear oluchi—

the light is blinking rapidly on the black boxy answering machine. your room seems bigger than before and i am still planning to read some of those robert jordan books of yours. yesterday at the used bookstore where i was browsing the mysteries to "stall reality" (they are really not mysteries at all, they just employ death as the plot mistress but are unable to grasp its mystery at all)—well the point is, things were calm down here for a while and the world was little. i want to be big like you. or i want you not vast, not dead, not gone, but human small and here. i am so selfish. that is what i really want. to see you again. to oil your scalp. to hear you walk in the door, say *ma i'm home*. give me a chance to say *welcome home son*. or when leaving, *don't forget your hat*. what do you wear out there? i wish you could have taken your new shoes with you. i'm so proud of you. i'm so sorry for the way you died. i miss you all the time. even before, i missed you. out there, one time, some different men said: *"shake for me girl, i wanna be your backdoor man."* who dat you love. 5/18/03 *ha ha haha ha ha ha hahaha ha ha ha ha hah ah ha hahha aha haahh ah ha ha ahh* double face days   murdering days

hyena days   days of last regrets

haunting days   the days of times   the storied days

ease dropping days   days of second listening

double days   crossroad days   days of disguise

breathing days   dream days   two-timing days

days of gasp   forget me not days   crossover days

last night days   fist days   thirst days once upon a time we walked to the corner store

      the man put the chili from the crock pot   get help from
the inside   next week   aesthetic of references
     once you've got a comrade   what a wonderful day   girl girl
boy boy   ice cream sandwiches   next week   and on his farm he had
some pigs   on the inside and you know the secret of transport
we hereby have come together under the gorgeous teardrops lessons and passages

traveling to and away
then i was carrying the baby in my arms   and as i said that the energy shifted
again

                                        desire is not
clean is not clean is not clean is not clean is not clean is not desire
sing and once again leaving   this impenetrable filmy mist that surrounds
stay let go no stay here in me a little longer keep you here in my body a little longer on
earth
i didn't expect to be in this temple
i want you to tell me things like it's so beautiful out here you'd tell me when you tell me
things
it's your innocence and complexity that floors me
are you my ancestor   my angel   my guide   my chosen one   my
baby, yes, even
now
in this cycle of little deaths   even now   my baby   a sweet love

second sight days   yellow shirt days   vandal days

days of let me go   days of ahhhhhhh   giving time days

little days   days of not now then if   traveling days

        there goes my baby walking by days

what days   days of oracle   hush mouth days

aching days   be good days   mistaken days

don't let the sun catch you crying days   go days   grace days

        thank you days   silly girl days   beautiful boy days   hatchet

days   days of clear sight   greedy days

the dream a site
recovered stammer, tocology, tokos
jural hiatus
hydrated gesture
for example: i hold you

beautiful boys girls beautiful
beautiful girls boys beautiful
beautiful boys girls beautiful

i'm extending to you this oh
i'm extending to you this oh oh o ho
i'm extending to you this oh o
i'm extending to you this oh o oh o o
i'm extending to you this oh o o oh oh
oh oh oh oh oh oh oh ohoh oh oh oh oh oh ohho oh oh oh oh angels

**how you
livin how
you livin
how you
livin how
you livin
how you
livin how
you**

can you spare just one

        can you spare just one

                can you spare

just   one

keeping time with spirits   **how you livin**
keeping time with spirits   **how you livin**

                    how you livin
     all around me   **how you livin**
     all around me

            keeping time

who dem all come

my sweet loved one
my loved one   *whatcha name is*
all around me
all round   *whatcha name is*   *who dem all*

moving time

i have wrapped you in rose petals and clean sheets   beautiful boys girls beautiful
                                     beautiful girls boys beautiful
                                     beautiful boys girls beautiful

oh oh oh oh oh oh oh ohoh oh oh oh oh oh ohho oh oh oh oh angels

        whatcha name is   *who dem all come*

oh this little night is a fine time
i can see they bodies not bodies

how you
livin how
you livin
how you
livin how

whatcha name

always eyes not one both   *who dat dere*

i have bathed your feet and hair in the fifth chamber   *see youuuuuuuuuuuu*

walking in spirit
all the way up there

i have baptized your testes and stomach with eucalyptus kisses
i get to be all now mama i get to
be all now mama i get to be all now mama i get to be all now all now all now

who dat dem come who dat dem come dem come who dat dem come

45

in a clear eastern wind now

in a clear eastern wind

always eyes not one both   we have love we have love we have love we have love we have love we have love we have love we have love keeping time with spirits we have love we have love *i get to be all now* we have love we have love we have love we have love we have love we have love keeping time with spirits *who dat dem* those are some good walking shoes all the way up there by the river we have love we have love we have love we have saints are walking thru the open gate we have love we have love we have love who dem all come an arriving guard of angels, thusly coming to greet

cartography of ghosts
. . . And as a way to talk . . .
of temporality
the topography of imagination,
this body whose entry into the articulation of history as rapturous becoming
& unbecoming,
greeted with violence,
i take permission to extend this grace

Sumptuous, the wearied worldly things,
always in return

the first dream child was the dreamer of dreams

> *for i have been an exiled orphan in the bright*
> *world far too long*

the second dream child was the teller of tales

> *for sin should not have dominion over you for you are not*
> *under law but under grace (Romans 6:14)*

the third dream child the keeper of clouds

> *before us he presented himself in his one perfect body;*
> *did we see?*

the fourth dream child was the whisperer of woes

> *and a great grief hath walked unto my path,*
> *it has blocked my reception; i am no more a stranger*
> *here than i ever was, no more at home than i shall ever be, here on these*
> *high and slow roads*

the fifth dream who was the word the lance and the spear

> *as if all things had origins in delight*

the sixth dream child was the giggly goofy goose

> *oh mcdonald had a farm, ei ei o, and on his farm he had*
> *some bears, ei ei o, and on his farm he had white*
> *buffalo, ei ei o, and on his farm he had lions, ei ei o, and on*
> *his farm he had some elephants, ei ei o*

the seventh dream child was the custodian of the keys

if you have trouble with the locks, go to 868

the eighth dream child carried the one perfect body

"there, where all the people go, where she was
before, swimming along roads, flying off cliff tops, across oceans,
getting there"
(Patricia Grace)

the ninth dream child carried the hourglass of waking

everyone i've ever been, every lover i've loved, deceived, or
believed, haunts me, everyone i've ever been

the tenth dream child the articulator of ghosts

nights are like this

the eleventh dream child was the maker of memory

there is so much love here, i cannot speak   yet

the twelfth dream child was the generous extended hand and i took the child's hand and was led to the thirteenth dream child and the thirteenth dream child radiated light and fire and invited me on a journey, so

i walked through the radiant fiery light and walked to the tears
and when i arrived at the tears they rejoiced and sent me to the muses
so i went to the muses and told them my disappointments so the muses
consulted and sent me to the enchanted lords of clouds and

when i ascended to the clouds they recounted my worth and chanted my fears and the fears and clouds carried me to the anger which received me gently then i was to the forever dream and when i arrived in the forever dream my name had become another and i recognized myself in the face of the children and the dream children chanted *both/both* and i met all the ghosts who come and go still and the ghosts and the dream children took my hand and we plummeted down a long and narrow tunnel and when we landed we stood before the screaming hieroglyphic wall and the wall began to whisper, the wall was prayer, the wall was a sage, it sang

this child is the dream and
the dreamed child

this child is the love and
the loved child

this child is the visible unseen child

this child is the coming forth and
the going child

this child is the undead and
the living child

this child is the just and
the journeyed child

this child is the one and
the both both child

monarch days

                           choke days   proletarian days

voicing days

              milady days   cub days

              couvade days

micrometer days   flamy days

            gentle days

flamy days

            gentle days   testis days

            prompt book days   tertiary days

       ambassadress days   refrain days

premillennial days

            more days

\

come
whenever you have want of the body life
the water is warm
dream with me
sing with me for a while

and now, well now,
this insurgency is   be good days

visible   prayer   grace days

unseen

will it disappear if the bodies that produce i
                                    unseen

hush mouth days
        aching days
today if we was talking, we would speak of causality
                hing days
        oracle days
    be good days
        greedy days

oracle days
        still about visible days
        mistaken days

What does it mean for a culture to Act?
        and now, well now this action is prayer
HERE HAVE THEY STASHED THE POLITICAL VANDALS?
        where have the stashed the political van

the visible unseen

the absent visible body—writing comparable to guerilla tactics—to strike, retreat, in striking, to change the landscape, to alter the public, i.e. political, space, to force a discourse outside of the script, to flip the script—the body is present in the visibility of the language, in the style, in the technique(s) that inform the writing, but the actual body is coded, is phantom, is transient and nomadic, therefore evading not subjectivity, but ownership and control over that body, over the writing itself, since the author(s) are apparitions. who is the nomadic body, who by its very evasiveness, transmutes a stationary location? this body that is not a locatable physical subject. how does this kind of writer who has abandoned attachment to the *author* as a position that must be located in discursive proximity to its production, its writing, convert the very systems and conditions of language = producer, receiver?

When I first saw graffiti, I recognized in it an ugly ecstatic, a dialects of violence, a distortion of limbs, a hieroglyph. It was only later when I read the names of the dead that I then saw the path of ghosts charted there; its

narrative of loss for the visible unseen whose place in history has been fiction-
alized and rendered unseen under the totalizing glare of history.

if by definition writing as cultural activism is concerned with engaging
socio-political systems, then it is concerned with form as well as
content. graffiti uses collage, bold gestures, concerns itself with
fonts, stylistic conceits, concerns itself with not just its public
nomenclature, but in upsetting and reconstituting the visual forms of
public discourse, of public space. it advertises difference and
insurgency, illegality, vandalism, distraction not just in its placement,
but in its aesthetic, in its attention to the shape of the emotion, to the
act of naming.

. . . it reconstructs the lies . . .

as a form graffiti is in a constant state of tension
shifting its nomadic position spatially
transiently. it upsets, redistributes through combat

disassemblage, distortion.

the bodies insist on painting themselves in markets they seemingly have no legitimate right to.

in its refusal to disappear it forces a discourse in the public imagination we are forced to see what we would rather not,

to make sense of an encoded language that we cannot read on the level of meaning.

it irritates, forces its agency upon us, speaks outside and beyond semiotic reach.

that is, it is a glossary that shifts, mutates, has stable referents that are constantly and seemingly arbitrarily defined,

codified, and discarded.

Graffiti (fr GK -graph(os), something drawn or written, to diagram or chart) attempts to stage the impossible: to erase the essence of its own subjectivity. Graff is a cartography of ghosts, a mapping of elegiac rapture (the transporting of a person from one place to another, as in heaven) and rupture (the state of being broken open). Dwelling is a fiction of stasis.

complicating or troubling the position of the graff writer as phantom absent author is that we know very well that in fact the ghost is / was embodied, speaks to and through cultural

productions, specific identities, home communities, but still manages through encoding to

evade as it upsets and redistributes identities. each piece, each throw-up chronicles the days.

The notion of the past as being something done with, a look-back event, inhibits the possibility of reading graffiti as rapture, as rupture. If graffiti posits history as always in the process of becoming undone. And memory, then, is history's mistress. That is, memory does not stand outside or apart from the becoming and undoing that is history. If we can accept that history and memory are lovers, then we can understand the desire for the bodylife to extend its grasp beyond mediated temporality. Because what is the body, if not also a complex temple, an unstable site through which to negotiate subjects, materiality, economies, gods, and modes of representations? The site where we are all already belated.

meditations (redemption chant)

"The right ending is an open door you can't see too far out of. It can mean exactly the opposite of what you are thinking."
—MICHAEL ONDAATJE

love me and holding.
love me and holding.
love to me and holding.
love to me and holding.
endearment.   endearment.
endearment.   endearment.
endearment.   endearment.
same act as dying. as being reborn.
breathe deep. then deeper still.
i have already forgiven myself my angers. i have already walked into the field of
my darkest angers.
now remember this when i am there in it now.
when i am there in it now. when i am there in it now.
remember this. when i am there. in it now. this when i am there. in it. now.
this when i am there in it now remember this when i am there in it now
grace grace grace grace grace grace grace grace grace grace grace grace
grace grace grace grace grace grace grace grace grace grace grace grace
grace grace grace grace grace grace grace grace grace grace grace grace
grace grace grace grace grace grace grace grace grace grace grace grace
grace grace grace grace grace grace grace grace grace grace grace grace
gracious self you have revealed yourself worthy
gracious self you have revealed yourself compassionate
gracious self you have revealed

gracious self you have revealed yourself
gracious self you have revealed
gracious self you have revealed yourself
gracious self you have revealed
gracious self you have revealed yourself
gracious self you have revealed
walk walk walk walk walk walk
walk and keep spirits
walk in spirit walk in spirit walk in spirit walk in spirit walk in spirit walk in
spirit walk in spirit
walk in spirit walk in spirit walk in spirit walk in spirit walk walk wake wake
wake
wake in compassionate awareness
wake in compassionate awareness
wake in compassionate awareness
wake in compassionate awareness
wake in compassionate awareness
my shame has left home my shame has renounced its false form.
one red smear of lipstick
is all i require most days. one red smear. i know
what color the blood comes out.
no suicides noun.   no suicides noun.
            no suicides noun.
                        no suicides.   no suicides.
noun. noun. noun.
verbs will follow.
verbs will follow.
disrupt the arrangement.
magic intervention
magic intervention
not too tired to know what i know.

yo yea

not too tired to know what i know

yo yea

not too tired to know what i know

yo yo yea yo

not too tired to know what i know

yo yo yo yo yo yea yo

not too tired to know what i know

yo yo yo yo yo yea yo

not too tired to know what i know

yo yo yo yo yo yea yo

not too tired to know what i know

yo yo yo yo yo yea yo

yo yo yea yo yo yo yo yea

the poplar trees live here sweet loved one

the hard ass edge lives here sweet loved one

the space of not forgetting lives here sweet loved one

the space of everyday is precious lives here sweet loved one

the space of everyday is precious lives here sweet loved one

the space of yea yo yea yea yea yo yo lives here sweet loved one

the space of everyday mundane beauty lives here sweet loved one

sweet loved one

the space of tearful abundance lives here sweet loved one

the space of not knowing all knowing lives here sweet loved one

the space of proper warrior spirit lives here sweet loved one

the space of proper warrior spirit lives here sweet loved one

the space of joyful voice lives here sweet loved one

the space of joyful warrior stance lives here sweet loved one

the space of ghosts lives here

sweet loved one

sweet

the space of morning redemption lives here sweet loved one
the space of mourning redemption lives here sweet loved one
the space of morning redemption lives here sweet loved one
the space of morning
the space of mourning
the space of morning
the space of morning
the space of mourning
the space of mourning
the space of morning
the space of mourning
the space of mourning
the space of morning
looked out the window at the pure white snow
i was not rejoiceful
i looked out the window at the baby tearful snow
        i moored   i mourned
        i morned like a visiting rainbow
i looked thru the window and saw the entire world on the deck
i looked thru the window and saw the entire world bedeckcd
i looked thru the window and saw inlaid jade
crystals and rose quartz lining
the walkway of knowing not knowing
lining the walkway of knowing not knowing
saw smooth black beautiful stones
some jagged knife blades
some bones of dead
some laser sharp recriminations
some perfections
some asking like the little duck where
their mommy has gone some knowing already

some in levi's jackets 1973 santa monica gap
some in lesser uniforms of insufficiency
some armies some bloated tongues some expelled cadets
some grandmothers two white braids choking their heads
some grandfathers incontinent and stumbling some
children displaying loyalty to batteries rusted and impotent some red
engines racing to disaster
some like familiars
holding the space
holding the space some with no judgment holding the space
on white horses holding the space
some of tobacco stained legacies holding the space
some of considerable weight holding the space
some of wealth and poverty holding the space
some of contention holding the space
some of neglect holding the space
some of misspelled surnames holding the space
some of tinker toy consistency holding the space
some of sweet surrender holding the space
some of babies dreamed and abandoned holding the space
some of lost tears holding the space
some of two faces holding the space
some of twin hydra holding the space
some of buddha love holding the space
some of no mothers holding the space
some of demonic diminutive holding the space
some of fancy dress holding the space
some of simple tastes holding the space
some of sons of midnight holding the space
some of someday my prince will come holding the space
some of decimated towers twin holding the space

some of discontinuous abandonment holding the space

some of tired eyes holding the space

some of false teeth holding the space

some of talcum powdered bottomed purity holding the space

holding the space   holding the space   holding the space

          holding the space

Fib #7809

Disjuncture}1

the difference between chicken breast fillets and ground turkey should be obvious I hadn't noticed it until the kitten cried.

glimpse #245: whatever's happening to us seems to be really strange but the strangest thing is nobody seems to be in charge of it.

Disjuncture}2

don't dream that I don't dream of you. sometimes I do. I'm tired was just a statement. no reason to doubt veracity. or to sleep until three in the afternoon is normal if the sounds from the fire hydrants kept you awake all night. paris must be a different city than this one. I did walk on cobblestones once but it seems like that was baltimore. I don't know anything about that place. your tongue has an obvious attachment to things that taste slightly salty. I don't think I'd feel as sexy in a hair weave. or the skin of a lover past her prime.

glimpse #98: it was the most intimate thing me laying my head on your back a leathered parcel you won in a crap shoot thirty-nine years ago.

Disjuncture}3

now that has got to take the cake. a forest should be an actual location or a storybook ideal of evil. like the shadows of denver streets after 10 p.m. when you died I thought everything would change for the better but things just got worse for a while. she was sent here to un-invent the family. an alliance to Mondays. a plotless wonder.

glimpse #456: I thought you said no but that was just another kind of unknowing of *what to do* as if this calls for some definitive action this slow falling away from one another.

glimpse #56: I thought you'd tell me something definitive why johnny can't read & then it would all be settled.

Disjuncture}4
you asked me where the passion went as if I should be able to trace its source to a gully or exclamation point. as if clever were a disguise I could shrug off at any whimsical point in the plot revealing myself really just a plain girl. a workhorse in sensible low heeled shoes shopping for the family's daily rutabagas at a predestined location while donkeys bray loaded down with trade.

glimpse #098: if woman is a false category then I've just made all this up.

Disjuncture}5
salty unlike sexy doesn't get in the way of things when you need to invent a letter to write to someone you hardly know. it could just be my old-fashioned selfish impulses at work here but I wanted to see the squirrel swing itself off the tree ledge down into the snow drift below. a reinforcing syntax. double negative. I don't know nobody. the first statement of truth: dear:
a disarming endearment. false negative. we don't have anything in common. or john, we hardly knew you. I wanted to wear the body you'd taken on as a thirty-something woman curled in the leather barstool of the five and dime novel.

glimpse #234: when finally the fairy princess felt brave enough to leave the castle walls she only made it as far as the local seven-eleven but even that was better than nowhere.

glimpse #98: it was the most intimate thing me laying my head on your back a leathered parcel you won in a crap shoot thirty-nine years ago.

Disjuncture}6
dear: i'm sorry I didn't return your call right away but the days just seem to run into each other like one endless sentence and besides I didn't want to talk in the voice you would expect of me.

glimpse #56: I thought you'd tell me something definitive, like why johnny can't read & then it would all be settled.

Disjuncutre}7
what if all the people are getting ready "cause there's a train coming." a code in which we all speak like mtv. apparent acronyms that take up little emotional space. nafta. nwa. a mode of thought that brings everything neatly together in a master script.

glimpse #88: I want the drama of a declarative statement like if I break your heart again I'll kill myself but is too early for all that the sun is a vain mistress squalored on the dirt eaten grass outside this frame & besides it's ridiculous to say good-bye with an idiom.

glimpse #456: I thought you said no but that was just another kind of unknowing of *what to do* as if this calls for some definitive action this slow falling away from one another.

Disjunture}8
you broke my heart. now that's a handy idiom. I call for a language of shared possibilities. not the limited inferences of mother lover car cake run. disfigurements in expected speech. a man of the people.

glimpse #097: if there is really no such location called female then we've just made all this up.

glimpse #245: whatever's happening to us seems to be really strange but the strangest thing is nobody seems to be in charge of it.

Disjuncture}9

false alliances to activisms like insisting on a female gynecologist or buying black or drinking zapatista grown coffee makes me feel better. and because I feel better by extension perhaps the world is now a slightly better place. like carefully plotting all appointments in the daily calendar masks a slight quivering in the fingers when I think of IT. the antithesis of lying on one's rusty dusty.

glimpse #98: it was the most intimate thing me laying my head on your back a leathered parcel you won in a crap shoot thirty-nine years ago.

Fib #99

walking early this cold morning when I could no longer bear
the simple and sad gloom that laced my discontent, the sky
as grimace or some kind of anguish: similar to a woman's
face: in this case, entirely arbitrary woman's: woman as
totalizing term: the essential grimace: a falling away from
youth: a mirror cold recognition, slight panic, tubercular
temporal, the unconscious reaching for the breast, a
reassurance: sexy this intimacy of gesture = a kind of *holding
one's own meaning.* what if when it finally betrays me or I
it I am unready to let go. the most ordinary happenings
negotiate their own permanence: this I think I will
remember when I am there in it now.

Fib #9037

nice is i suppose another town
nice is i suppose another town

wish the troops didn't know it was there
it's groovy there's a game plan on the other continent

i had peas for dinner when i was small they were green round

and something like i imagine death if i am the sum of all the broken

the men in fatigues would not massacre the family i visited them it was such a hard
journey in nighttime space the sky was disappeared and the floors damp
with browned blood of those whose names escape anyone's national media

i wish it were another day already

we could be having vodka tonics in an apartment and not even pretend to need
witnesses

my mother was here for a while in this script not the hero or villain you
invented once
upon an oops there it is this is another dirge and i
imagined it something different

suitable for political rallies when death and shame
were soothing and you could overhear conversations from temporary bedroom
where you resided and they spoke in terms you would dismiss

or love who knows like the mother thing it's yes or no the silly opposites hello hello

hello it's me said a voice from somewhere else and it was late but maybe not too

(who could know, it's those crazy christians on the radio again

i'd like all the stone butches to wave their hands in the air right now, wave em like they just don't care

(it seems to be unfortunate but true; corporate spell check does not recognize you

we are all too young to remember this

fib #198291

•

Eating a Banana Muffin, the great _____ celebrates finally finishing.
Reports on dolphins.
"Make a poem about me and take it to the workshop."
We've almost completed a decade.

•

Of the expansive vocabulary.
Answer his question with a smile as if the question has only been
asked to illicit an affection.
A straw in transparent plastic wrapper comes attached.
Two women walk by.

•

Sitting here in my little apartment I come to an agreement.
I cut out *National Geographic* Africans for first birthday card collage.

•

He keeps right on eating.
Beautifully inscribed tongue.
We're afraid to say we laugh sometimes.
The waiter repeats a litany, five flavors of soda.

•

He comes attached.
Concentrate on events.
I hear the sound of boys upstairs.
Innocent snip clip of toy guns.

•

Fallen but not dismissed.
Sunsets December on Coney Island.

•

"My name ain't midget."
Short film about a three-year-old's trip to the laundromat.
Images of him like sequential postcards parading down Lafayette.
Someone alerts me to the culprit.

•

The love I know.
Using his little back muscles he sits right up, eats my arm.
That is what I have to offer.
His smile sweeter than a midday honey lollipop on Venice Beach.

•

Spirit is another person.
Neo-traditional forms in which case a constant attunement is required.
I was once dreaming.
I recall a group of people me included.

•

I suppose we are sabotaging cars as they come by.
When I saw him I just hugged him and hugged him.
For the first time in two days we laugh sincerely with each other.
Things surface finally with no convenient distractions.

•

I am in the dawning of a hip new awareness.
It must be terrible to want things.

·

He watches the pen as if seriously contemplating its validity.
This rainy Saturday in March.
I wake without you.
I'm sure it is nothing personal that the rain is falling now, it's falling all
over Oakland.

·

We should all learn magic.
"Follow the fellow who follows the dream," her father tells her that.
This feels like rough paper, like a certain kind in elementary school.
_____ does a magic trick today and calls it homeopathy.

·

_____ is so much himself.
The why of some thing,
He repeats the question.
We both are awakening from a three-hour nap.
We are talking about eating after the seminar.
Before that I am walking or riding around in what appears
to be a strange country.

·

If this is not the case then I certainly don't want to entertain an illusion.
Where I live there is the constant sound of birds, sparrows I think.
It might look like the country or just an expansive open.
Things are looking quite good this Thursday mid-May.

•

I know he is in there because someone spits up baby spit.
I'm stuck writing in a journal about how young I feel.

•

All this energy is pulsating in her.
That is the most beautiful thing I have heard in some time.
Plays a xylophone, one that moves I do believe.
The last week of our Bay Area experience I buy him another
pair of white shoes even smaller than the ones he had.

•

This business of finding words is very difficult.
I love you _____.
_____ gives a goofy chuckle, bites into his muffin, rests his black
stocking foot on my bare left foot.
My typewriter motor buzzes, for fifteen hours straight I write
without light.

green fibs

i am thinking about good intentions
playing the arenas: how new gender identities upset petunias
shifting thru sand to find the silver thread
blackening the dialogue: a philosophical topic posted

most of the truth has to do with the partial dream
in other words: show yourself
an adornment is what the *i* is:
name the want

in jackie's bed the voices said release shame
in echo, in stream, in judgment, in craft
candles burn for shango
think i'll stay here, act like lovers do

he's got that bored, overly exposed to a trivial world american look
the tallness of the woman was important
not fully engaged
challenge of holding new forms

i am walking down a carnival
not beautiful, not that smart, not that blessed, but a tenacious hostage
what does it mean to be a postcolonial subject
an i in a category that as of yet is i not idaho

at first i was lost but now i am found
a natural chick i think as i look at the receptionist

in her natural gray clogs
history could articulate the ooze
should i stay or should i go
a groovy coyness my body asking what i see
new york family simmering in red whore light
to fail again a promise not intended to keep

to do something that is detrimental to the dreamer
"well i had a dream that i had some friends and some girls
from my class were running down the hallways and we
caught them and we took them back to the stage"

grass, canvas, walls, bodies, boxes, memory, sidewalks
offer a range of possibilities for addressing subjects
as i was falling downstairs i did not feel any shots

which leads to the other collusion: is it not the action that's important
what she want
a very kind indian man drew me a map then shapeshifted into sister
i is a journal

russia, kiev, ice cream, donald duck, texas, sophia loren, mao's little red
book, the ironing lady, dialectical materialism, stax records,
supermarket fine china
bards are the official grief scribes
saw her earlier at the coffee shop she looked real boy

people don't know how to chill but we do
the delusional mind
twilight i am sitting on a skin scurried away
preceding final darkness

close with a ritual of acknowledgment
ghosts and gods honor the invisible
look there's eileen myles reading poetry in a laundromat
people doing the rope exercise

the show title: vicious children and zoe in *i am a computer*
a new support group for still queer ex-dykes
dred scott decision
hospital appointment at 2:00

if memory is the act of bearing witness
if jesus was born at midnight
if la la la la la la la la lalalallllaaaaaaa
then the dream is a friend driving us somewhere

my hand casts a shadow across the page and i am
writing above my shadow
tender relationships
i meet a man i identify as outcast who speaks of the negro inside me
those horses we rode off the gulf of mexico sweet

and you are my brother
rain, disappointment, coal, jupiter, and a kiss
i need a lot and am no longer ashamed of this vulgarity
actually the words don't have to be too big, just the concepts obscured

a hard time coming forth is weeping hour
9 symbolizes completion of a natural order
new york a sleepy town yawning awake at noon

inflammation of vagina, dizziness, insomnia, anxiety, secondary male
characteristics, joint pain, eye problems, thirst, hair loss, breast tenderness
only time and the next phone call will tell
i keep dreaming of water, practice the art of iridescence

his face clouds and he says no
everybody is discharging so everybody is innocent
evil unveiled itself in a single avowal
i can't live where i can't dream

it's as if there is no waiting space
the word sex is not a sexy word
some friends of mine came by and got caught up
in whatever they were doing

vaginas destabilize a voyeuristic master narrative
i'm really going to need some nonfiction
in the journey of this dream i meet a man
i plan to ask

stinky from the sloppy house across the street borrows some flour
fanny predicts i'll write a famous novel and get $172,000
julia studies feminist theory in college
marcia, dona, marguerita, & donna walk to the store to get now 'n' laters
i'm thinking to myself: "don't, those waters will betray you"
akilah's talking about the three conditions for conversing
with one's angel
tommy is sitting in the corner singing "the world loves a winner"
luch says, yes those times work perfectly i just got your e-mail
rik is manifesting abundance

soccoro's got to be at the foot clinic at 9 A.M.

anki says, "west village, all the way to the hudson, between 10th & 14th"

erika and lynne are sitting on a curb watching elephants go by

someone is waving at all sentient beings everywhere

michael ondaatje says: "he slipped back into my memory as accidentally
as a smell"

joe thinks it's happy martin luther king jr. day

zoran says these heavens aren't big enough for both him and jesus

jerry springer's on the tv deconstructing whiteness

three big women do ritual, curl purple silken streams of cloth from their
mouths, wrap

three unbroken white eggs in the cloth, kneel in prayer,

sing, "wading in the water, wading

in the water children, wading in

the water, god's gon' trouble the waters"

i'm thinking this is going to be a long day, living in reseda

our good day

1.

i don't desire narrative structure but i want you to hear this story in a way that you'll "get it." like once upon a time.

2.

"I desire the purity of milk."
and once again i didn't know what s/he was/not talking about, but it sounded like something believable.

3.

a normative reality wanted to inject itself into the lover's vocabulary.

4.

everyone's gotten so smart in the post-identity age. they disjunct. and because i don't know what to say, i pretend i am confused and committed and popular like ani difranco

5.

this is a travel story. about how a boy and girl leave home separately, go off to play dress up and other important games in the big world. (working title) our good day.

6.

i forget the party line, i think it has to do with
her he ate him she ate him he ate her.
and to think, i was attached to his breasts.
i forget the party line, i think it has to do with "margarine."

the ant does not know he's an ant although apparently
the crocodile and the scorpion do.
the alternative would, would be in brooklyn.

7.

the way i desire to remember this story honors the rain, but not the
facts. memory is a devious bitch, the unfaithful lover, the shifting face
of the adulterer. it's what i have after gary died. a long time ago i was
young, really young in the american way, unsuspecting of sorrow and
death. gary was young too. in the american way, youth bears a
resemblance to a certain exulted ignorance and though the young
speak volumes and know many things, we are not expected to
remember those things later, to tell the story as if cultural memory
were historical documentation. the chronology of things—first
second third and so on, sequential dates—those are the optional
orders and since after a while, nobody really expected either of us,
gary or me, to make good, we didn't bother to keep the daily journal.

8.

"Something about the futility of seduction comes to mind here . . .
if i can seduce the 'Other,' if i can trick the Other into adoring the
promise of love, i can make a lie convincing. a charade exists in the
'court and spark.' game that ultimately comes undone, that unveils
itself as human, gracious, base, mundane even."

9.

what if you were really afraid and the world betrayed you or you it
and really there is nothing you can do about it. not betrayal in the
literal sense of desertion or denial, but the way a balloon popped at a
party catered to five-year-olds in a time of monochrome, unexpected
the way they do sometimes, when you are happy and bouncing it

around. then pop. there it goes and it is nothing. the quality of air untrustworthy. betrayal, like your mom isn't god. not really something devious or planned, more like an arrival. perhaps a truth. sooner or later you'd figure it out. who could be god?

10.

I desire to hold it (someone for my own simple "pleasure"). to not suffer the loss of departure of the Other as a "self" outside of my desire of/for that Other. it's self reflective. or object referent. that is, i adore the object (my love) so i must contain it so i can derive pleasure and power from my own gaze. because perhaps one likes the way a bird flutters around in a cage. because pictures are pretty or functional or value-based or because that's the weakness of the sad coward. because that's the diverted power of the landless.

11.

i want to call him victor but his name was gary and i was in love with him. i met him on a street in new york i wish i could remember which one. if i could then i could do that novelistic thing and map the narrative for you but i can't remember and it was in july or june and it was hot and night and he had on a bette midler tee-shirt and the tee-shirt had blood stains on it and it seemed slightly incongruous that this black guy had on a bette midler tee-shirt but it all makes sense now that there is postmodernism and i am a postcolonial subject sometimes. he was walking toward me it's nineteen eighty-four and we don't know what aids is yet but soon we will but we're not there yet it's nineteen eighty-four and we're free still or stupid and i am walking too so perhaps i am walking toward him. we can be heroes. and that is that. david bowie will be important in this story too but that is later, in august, when boombox will be a cultural marker of symbolic significance though i may forget so perhaps you will remember that boombox is supposed to be important in this story. though later. in august. not now. this is the beginning.

12.

they are making up themselves. they put on makeup. they make up with each other. they get high and fight and play and fight then they make up. they learn how to cut. cut skin and hearts and bread and ropes and other important things that they can cut. they learn to use different cutting tools. lasers and words and scissors and fingernails and paper and they papier-mâché. they make things with paper and cutting tools but not the way they were taught in kindergarten. but sometimes like that.

13.

"have some white bread with mayo on it and spaghetti" or "we're eating like we're poor cause we're poor."

14.

there were graveyards placed on coffee tables around the house.

15.

i like to think my father loved to sing though i know it isn't true. what he loved was shadows, the grayness filtering through the slits of venetian blinds at midmorning infiltrating the unlit living room where the green couch sat in a room tight with absence. what i think he loved were the records he played over and over. miles davis forlorn, charlie parker, bird, sarah vaughn, song. all the others. i didn't know what time it was. once when i was sitting there on the green couch, small and alert because he spoke to me, he said, "do you know why they call him 'bird'?"

i didn't know and shook my head in a way i hoped would signal an intent. that i didn't know in the way i didn't know most things then because i was small. i thought he would tell me, but it was another quiz to which there was an answer, but i was supposed to figure it out myself. later when things were lighter. los angeles was heavy with scars of a thing called watts riots. we saw it on the television one night when the grandmother we called mother was visiting from st. louis and the riots stuff, that was another thing that i knew there was an answer for, a reason, but i didn't know what that could be either. just that it was important and was somewhere in the black and white faces of those negro men and a few women the camera caught on a street somewhere nearby that housed burning buildings and everything seemed wet like it had been raining. the bodies on the screen, unanchored defiance, a strange fright. this was somehow connected to why they called him "bird." i'd like to think my father loved my mother but i knew even then that that wasn't true. my mother gave my father a look she'd often scrawl on her face, her painted lips turning down slightly, her voice over-enunciating hard consonants, when he said, "good for them." she said she didn't think that was necessary in front of the children. i liked how she seemed to think the children were something to protect. i know she thought by protecting us we'd be safe and make it.

i wanted to make it too for a while but then i changed my mind. that was even before i met gary. i think changing my mind had something to do with always being able to sit anywhere i wanted on the bus. i remember the other times before when some people called "we" couldn't, sit anywhere on the bus, because i read about it and saw the movies, but not really. i don't really recollect it at all. but maybe i will, later in the story. when boombox and david bowie both will be important. important.

16.

there is a perception of knowing but i think it really just is a kind of avoidance in the eyes, a buried utterance.

17.

this is a happy story but first i want to tell you about the shape of the incredible sadness. a porn movie you volunteer for. unpaid. intended. charitable. the sadness has that shape. a moon misted over. a stubborn dyke at the bar prepping an imaginary desire long past his prime. or an orphan. a korean orphan adopted by a nice suburban couple in orange county or one imported from bosnia never from the congo. it's a sadness that takes its place in an unoccupied region of your heart. even though you've seen duplications of what the heart is supposed to look like and you may have seen x-rayed type replications or even the actual heart from an autopsied body, it doesn't really look like that in your imagination. it looks like the hearts on a valentine's day card or one of those you made from construction paper in third grade when the teacher was nice to you and you wrote a story about you don't know what and she said it was good and you felt visible. the sadness is that shape.

18.

all the people who have lied are walking down bleeker street including me and all the people have lied sometime and so have i so it's appropriate that i am walking down bleeker street. i'm happy. i'm young. i'm making stuff up.

feral femina

headless breasts. imaginary eye. object. objectify.
objection. abject. abrupt. disruptive image.
                    she opens out to a blank space
who you be woman   who you be
clean carefully between the toes. lesson number one. walk.
one insult after another.
subject.
subjectivity. subjective. this is 62nd street. that's frothy white milk.
perspective of the seeing subject.
                    the loved body
obscenity of tongue. encoded. something posed and vile. this language
of absence. of agency. of a woman. just an ordinary woman.
daring speech.
yellow picket fence teeth.

She bit because she loved
She bit because she desired the act of taste
She bit to symbolize language.
She bit who she was not.

unobtainable idea. a speaking woman. object of the commodified gaze.
comic(al) subject.
                    she does not pose as herself
an arm imitates itself. breasts framed in gauze.
imaginary   *loved body*.
object installed for performance. headless woman.

a left arm masturbates the air. toneless woman.
a right arm draped over a divan.
nipples distended hunger. framed. headless woman. headless thing.
stomach obscene. nasty adjectives.

> *fascination being only the extreme of detachment*

site of eros. of forgot. of sneer. of supplication. of form.
of oppositional imagination. of desire.
of forget. of geography. of debasement. of vilification.
of mother. of fear. of agency. of speech. of forget.

language is a skin
memory is a skin
forgetting is a skin
lie is a skin
fear is a skin
desire is a skin
tongue is a skin
doubt is a skin
whip is a skin
absence is a skin.

dream

I dream of paralysis, of being paralyzed.
it's 6 a.m. or approximately,
the patient morning rests under eyelids,
crunch of dried venial leaves mime
a rapist's rasp outside on gray patio.
I use the machine to kiss you,
something mumbled replaces.
it's still too early, earlier than the beginning of this,
(is that a knife you dream)
a knowing that intimates less.   like that girl,
in the movie. you remember her. killer on
the run.

kill

then you get the sadness & you go to sleep for a while
   they work as moles in the mine shafts of peru   where
   their size makes them indispensable, and when their lungs
   give out they end up in unmarked graves
the special negro subverts the newly invented escaped slave   *they*
   defend order as if they own it, even though they're only tenants
   overwhelmed by high rents and the threat of eviction
special in their distress they distress me i am all ready   oh   how
   my desire insults the script   i am a whip   i wimp
   fuck you   foucault who
not you. those who never heard of fela and pretend   they   understand
   globalization
i already ate you and it was a satisfying meal dig it though i
hate you contingently i'd eat you again   yummy   turn
on the underground railroad channel   without   speech   i
   would be insane yo   if with speech just distracted.   it's
   disdained   difference   say it with a french
accent to get the difference   *there are investments of desire that*
   mold and distribute power   tell yo mama   that   you   really
   intend to find an identity by monday   yeah.
as if the form carries the fantasy   let's say women are
   homeless in the world
narratives of insufficiency that play themselves out as "i am rejecting the
   other"
i should go now   i think you need to walk down a block where
you are the deepest motherfucker on the block   it's   not

my block   as a kind of subjective fiction. *time lag keeps alive the*
making of the past. there was

an invisible binder   something   kept   gender   performance
contained   conscripted. as if all the twenty-somethings
had just finished reading judith butler   then the shadows
ultimate betrayers. how words distort their meanings straight
from the horse's mouth. the delusion of the special negro
how busy the transgressions today   *the stone butch has the*
dubious distinction of being

defined by what practices she does not engage in. is there any
other sexual identity   defined by what a person will not do?
the choir boys disrobed and pretty   i must love the world so much.
my self an adventure in it   i dreamed brother marc   last   night.   we
could still call this story "tracing the source of evil's sorrow."
the naming of the coming forth

strange surface night. it felt so sexy waking up third
the horse people live in their world and the poets live in their world.
i'm hearing a dance of birds   the dreamer dreams to be
loved loving the lover dreams to be the dreamer   who   is   dreaming
himself into another state of loving

another more perfect dream   oh let's go shout at the wolf now
my impossible body   *finally that vague feeling of discovery*
becomes very

clear so that almost no doubt remains you become one with the subject.
that is when i am the unbutch fag girl   opulent here in
the   sadness of my heart   i'm walking with
a young dark hair girl   we're going   to   a   different
place. *three ways to skin a cat   how to get over the hump.*
secret agent man's real identity.   lovely thieving writers
a haunting, you could say.   i fear the state may come
inappropriately into my home seize all my last season ex-lovers

find my body a crime.
the words all over the floor. a moon over an ocean
    we are swinging in levi's and corduroys   the word "cool" means
    something else and a white tee shirt will do
for the girl. a boot or low heel. every scuff mark   a map taking me
    before the memory judges   i like that dress on a mannequin.
    disrobe and give it to me
i will play dead
is this love is this love is this love that i'm feeling.

dear matthew shepard,

last night i dreamed deboned fish,
seems i've been dreaming
ideas in things for weeks now.
gracious dead ones enter me, they
name me. i thieve
their garments, mime their tongues, wear their
lesions and rope marks.
i scare myself like
a scarecrow did me when i was in little
body, seeing one for the first time
i think it was in east texas in '74, or maybe
in the land of oz.
(is that how it happens, like fade
aways & superimposition of images,
places transpose into simpler times,
familiar loved faces float in & out,
your mother's eyes maybe,
your near-corpse caressed by an
unbeckoned sweetness,
the boy you were going to meet any
day now, he soothes & lullabies your dangling body)
last night i dreamed frozen catfish,
i was trying to hold its icy form
it kept slipping away from me.
matthew, i feel like i'm slipping all
the time now, suspended between dream & death

is the way body
falls away
is the way
consciousness leaves

what did you fathom, matthew,
what resistance kept you alive,
through the hard night.
it was so fucking cold,
the sick act that hung you upon a sacrificial fence,
the normal boy american faces of the brutes
who played out their homicidal homophobia
on your beautiful
true form.
more often than not matthew, i've been
dreaming my beautiful true form will soon
fall away from me, and that nothing will be
finished, i won't be done
at all with worldly business.
& just as your death has become mine,
someone else will wear my broken bones,
wake trembling from sleep,
try to get the work done.

raw fish. raw fish everywhere

—————————,

how do you speak of children without memorializing them
or lying or praising a small limb you rubbed lotion on once as if it were
stuck in time and the boy has grown toward manhood but the mother
still stays in a rerun of another hallway another house another time like
i could say something now and go back and make any small hurt
or great betrayal disappear like a booboo covered by a band aid or this is
all silly he is on the journey from the lineage of intentional gypsies
a fate is a gift and i can listen to you grow stronger with glorious
discontent you a body still growing and forming itself semi-perfect
precious already this is sappy mothers can never really write of sons
and get it right we are too much writing about our own small
dilapidations as we tally their gains

_____,

and tenderly you want to touch his skin. to specify the moment of desire. you want to touch his face. the contours of the cheekbone rising above his left jaw. skin so pimply, smooth beneath. you want to breathe clarity into his face. the words just escape. unedited hoes or generous mothers, more like tears. incapable of apportioning themselves in dichotomous boxes. you say to him, precious child of your imagination and that carnal thing biology books in eleventh grade speak of called "the uterus" (you still believe the stomach is the holding site, no matter what they say, no matter how many teaching assessments you may have passed, no matter how many decades later, you still tend to say stomach . . . and you don't know why you say "tend," like "tend to your bizness lit girl" or tend to some unknown fire. your hand the object of knowing on his pimply brown cheek. a historical terrain passing beneath your touch. you want to tell him of the beauty of a boy you once knew. you called him brother. you sat with him on brick borders, dividing property lines. you want to tell him, for his whole generation. you want to say. you want to say. I once knew a baby boy. his confusion was much like yours. I loved him so deeply and skin, like yours, chaffed and ashen under a common household shower. his skin, the pimpled topography of battles, unknown soldiers, impervious little boy drummers, tears and hormones, like yours. I loved him much. I miss him much. my responsibility is not to you, as a little sister's would be. my responsibility to you, some almost twenty years after his death, is a mother's. not a baby sister's. how I miss being some precious forgotten boy's baby sister.

.

COLOPHON

A Toast in The House of Friends was designed at Coffee House Press, in
the Grain Belt Brewery's Bottling House near downtown Minneapolis.
Fonts include Caslon and Scala Sans.

FUNDER ACKNOWLEDGMENTS

Coffee House Press is an independent nonprofit literary publisher. Our books
are made possible through the generous support of grants and gifts from many
foundations, corporate giving programs, state and federal support, and through
donations from individuals who believe in the transformational power of litera-
ture. This book was made possible, in part, through a special project grant from
the Jerome Foundation. Coffee House Press receives general operating support
from the Minnesota State Arts Board, through an appropriation by the
Minnesota State Legislature and from the National Endowment for the Arts.
We receive major general operating support from the McKnight Foundation, the
Bush Foundation, and from Target. Coffee House also receives support from: an
anonymous donor; the Elmer L. and Eleanor J. Andersen Foundation; Bill
Berkson; the James L. and Nancy J. Bildner Foundation; the Patrick and Aimee
Butler Family Foundation; the Buuck Family Foundation; the law firm of
Fredrikson & Byron, PA.; Jennifer Haugh; Anselm Hollo and Jane Dalrymple-
Hollo; Jeffrey Hom; Stephen and Isabel Keating; the Kenneth Koch Literary
Estate; Seymour Kornblum and Gerry Lauter; Kathryn and Dean Koutsky; the
Lenfestey Family Foundation; Ethan J. Litman; Mary McDermid; Rebecca
Rand; the law firm of Schwegman, Lundberg, Woessner, PA.; Charles Steffey
and Suzannah Martin; Jeffrey Sugerman; the James R. Thorpe Foundation; Stu
Wilson and Mel Barker; the Archie D. & Bertha H. Walker Foundation; the
Woessner Freeman Family Foundation; the Wood-Rill Foundation; and many
other generous individual donors.

This activity is made possible
in part by a grant from the
Minnesota State Arts Board,
through an appropriation by the
Minnesota State Legislature
and a grant from the National
Endowment for the Arts. MINNESOTA
STATE ARTS BOARD

TARGET.

To you and our many readers across the country,
we send our thanks for your continuing support.

Good books are brewing at coffeehousepress.org

Printed in the USA
CPSIA information can be obtained
at www.ICGtesting.com
JSHW012012140824
68134JS00023B/2373